The Campus of LOVE

a sonnet cycle by
DUNCAN FRASER

Copyright © 2018 Duncan Fraser

The moral right of the author has been asserted.

Apart from any fair dealing for the purposes of research or private study, or criticism or review, as permitted under the Copyright, Designs and Patents Act 1988, this publication may only be reproduced, stored or transmitted, in any form or by any means, with the prior permission in writing of the publishers, or in the case of reprographic reproduction in accordance with the terms of licences issued by the Copyright Licensing Agency. Enquiries concerning reproduction outside those terms should be sent to the publishers.

Matador
9 Priory Business Park,
Wistow Road, Kibworth Beauchamp,
Leicestershire. LE8 0RX
Tel: 0116 279 2299
Email: books@troubador.co.uk
Web: www.troubador.co.uk/matador
Twitter: @matadorbooks

ISBN 978 1789013 191

British Library Cataloguing in Publication Data.
A catalogue record for this book is available from the British Library.

Printed and bound in Great Britain by 4edge Limited
Typeset in 11pt Minion Pro by Troubador Publishing Ltd, Leicester, UK

Matador is an imprint of Troubador Publishing Ltd

Contents

1.	Dogg's Hamlet, Cahoot's Macbeth	1
2.	CC2	2
3.	After the Show	3
4.	The Moment of Falling in Love	4
5.	Goof	5
6.	Terrifying Beauty	6
7.	Summa Theologica	7
8.	The Wave	8
9.	The Grange Wine Bar	9
10.	The MacBob	10
11.	Shrines and Omens	11
12.	Red Burgundy Check	12
13.	Bittersweet	13
14.	Mirroring	14
15.	The Ideal	15
16.	The A3 Lecture Theatre	16
17.	Inadequate Poet	17
18.	Pot Noodle Man	18
19.	The Christmas Card	19
20.	Spring Semester	20
21.	The All-Nighter	21
22.	Stirling University Campus	22
23.	Faintheart	23
24.	Wheelchair Guy	24

25.	The Doppelgänger	25
26.	Terrible News	26
27.	Peasant Slave	27
28.	Flightpath	28
29.	Santa Barbara	29
30.	Distance	30
31.	The Weird Coincidence	31
32.	Tranquillity	32
33.	Sixteen Long Months	33
34.	Roy Hattersley	34
35.	Extension	35
36.	Grand Canyon	36
37.	Continuous Assessment	37
38.	I Got You	38
39.	Paris, Texas	39
40.	The Library	40
41.	Dissertation	41
42.	The Friend	42
43.	Aborted Mission	43
44.	Windsurfer on Airthrey Loch	44
45.	I Finally Ask Her Out	45
46.	Unrequited Love	46
47.	Aftermath of Dreams	47
48.	The ASH Party	48
49.	Wallace Monument	49
50.	Paradise	50

1

Dogg's Hamlet, Cahoot's Macbeth

I must have seen her at the audition.
The first time I saw her must have been then.
But I can't recall her lovely face when
we read for parts with quiet ambition.

At rehearsals I had no suspicion,
as her character stepped into my ken,
that looks that erode susceptible men
had begun their amorous sedition.

The play was *Dogg's Hamlet, Cahoot's Macbeth*.
I was the Inspector, she the Hostess.
My main concern was to learn all my lines.

I feared drying on stage as much as death
and with this fear I did my love suppress.
I ignored my heart and its tiny signs.

2

CC2

After one good performance of the play,
the cast, relieved, repaired to CC2.
Actors making noise, posing as they do
as brilliant talents, putting drink away.

Though she could have sat with the loud and gay,
it was beside me that she took a pew.
I felt honoured but I secretly knew
it was by default my virtues held sway.

Bitter lemon was her poison of choice -
clearly, she was no party animal -
but I was keen to hear what she might share.

Before I could fall in love with her voice,
two of her friends spotted my new-found pal,
gathered her up and took her off somewhere.

3
After the Show

I was on the stage about to make tracks,
the last night over, the audience gone.
Cast and stagehands who were leaving anon
traded witty parting shots and wisecracks.

No actors had become amnesiacs,
thank God, and I felt pleased that I had shone.
But now, out of character, and withdrawn,
I stood as others zipped up anoraks.

Scared to appear too keen to get away,
we glanced at each other standing around
and I felt a real connection with her.

Perhaps I'm saying more than I should say;
yet my quietness and her lack of sound
harmonised right there in that theatre.

4

The Moment of Falling in Love

On a Sunday in 1982 -
October 24th to be precise -
I wake up sharp and without thinking twice
my soul just knows that I'm in love with you.

Fierce, exquisite feeling, so fresh, so new -
an intense awareness gained in a trice
that I am on fire, not frozen in ice,
that I'm no longer poor but well-to-do.

I picture her face, her beautiful face,
not just lovelier than all of the rest
but uniquely lovely, a single star.

My heart establishes the briskest pace.
I'm on target for a personal best.
This peasant thinks he can become the tsar.

5

Goof

Our paths have stopped crossing every day.
We no longer rehearse lines together,
we're no longer Hostess and Inspector,
no longer those characters in the play.

So why is it that this love comes my way
only now when I no longer see her?
Love's like an autocratic director
cutting lines that actors would love to say.

I was greatly praised for my performance
as the Inspector in the production
but I feel that the role was actor-proof.

Off the stage I have no such dominance.
And Love, a trickster fond of obstruction,
is, I fear, going to play with this goof.

6

Terrifying Beauty

At that time she was in her second year
and was living off-campus with two friends.
I seldom bumped into her at weekends
or knew the places where she might appear.

Time passed slowly when I didn't see her,
when I thought just glimpses would be godsends.
Those periods are long that a man spends
hoping the girl will stray into his sphere.

I soon discovered a rough rule of thumb;
she'd be somewhere around during the day
and probably be somewhere else at night.

Not yet the man I wanted to become,
I sometimes, on seeing her, turned away,
that sudden beauty filling me with fright.

7

Summa Theologica

I like how she moves, her carriage, her poise,
the modesty and restraint in her way
of walking; she wouldn't ever sashay
down a corridor of admiring boys.

This shy gait that her biggest fan enjoys
will sometimes, when she spots a friend, segue
into a kind of scurrying ballet
with small steps, folded arms and girlish noise.

In my Aquinas course we talk of God
and concepts like perfection and the good.
Images of her in my mind erupt.

Her lack of conceit is extremely odd.
Is there a secret she has understood -
how to be perfect while not being corrupt?

8

The Wave

I started to notice she'd have her lunch
in the lounge above the MacBob foyer.
I would often see her there at midday
dug in like an enemy in a trench.

It was impossible to reach the wench
in a seemingly adventitious way,
so outside of that lounge I had to stay
and be hit by frustration's avalanche.

As I would head down into the MacBob
among a crowd besieged by curried airs,
my hunger was for her propinquity.

I'd feel stymied, as helpless as a squab.
On a whim as I descended the stairs
I waved at her once. She never saw me.

9

The Grange Wine Bar

How many others are obsessed with her?
Could her lovely hair, her lips and her eyes
have gone unnoticed by the other guys?
I cannot be the only connoisseur.

She's unattached; I do not think I err.
That's not to say that others do not prize
this girl and also try to eulogize
her in their own twee poems and cris de coeur.

She has two female friends she is close to.
I see them at the wine bar in the Grange.
Their link with her is why they catch my eye.

I would like to know but I have no clue
why she seems to have no boyfriend. It's strange
I've never really seen her with a guy.

10

The MacBob

Often I sat alone in the MacBob
eating my dinner as dark descended.
Outside huge windows feral cats wended
their way to bowls of food and formed a mob.

If she was there at all, it was a job
to spot her. Would my famine be ended,
could this restaurant now be commended
because of her presence, would my heart throb?

I would gaze as far as I was able
at all the students who were dining there,
longing for my eyes to catch sight of her.

And sometimes, yes, at a distant table,
her long, unmistakeable, golden hair
turning all her surroundings to a blur.

11

Shrines and Omens

Certain places on campus were special.
The spots where she smiled were sacred to me.
Locations where we spoke to some degree
became shrines – this is so confidential.

My passion had turned me reverential.
All the sites in my mind's eye I could see
plotted in my lovestruck cartography.
No encounter was inconsequential.

Right there, in the cloakroom, just a few days
after the play, we met and talked a bit.
Once, on the link bridge there, we also spoke.

And I'd see omens, signs that would amaze
my enchanted mind, that I'd interpret
as that girl's common future with this bloke.

Red Burgundy Check

When I would spot her I would also note
the smart and beautiful clothes that she wore.
She had a dress sense I could not ignore
and her choice of attire would float my boat.

Whether it was jeans or jumper or coat,
she had a style that I came to adore.
I had seen no girl so well-dressed before
from her feet all the way up to her throat.

Padded gilets would look so good on her.
Her gloves fitted her like a glove – or gloves.
I loved her lovely scarlet polo neck.

I loved everything that she would wear.
But most of all I loved to see my love's
long, pleated skirt of red burgundy check.

13

Bittersweet

We pronounce *library* differently.
She uses only two syllables but
I pronounce it with three. I think I'll cut
my extra one out. Her way is lovely.

Her dainty handwriting impresses me.
A neat, flowing script like a perfect putt.
That blue ink packs a punch, an uppercut,
knocking me out with its exposed beauty.

I notice that it's through such mundane things
that the power of my love is revealed.
But as we part – an aftertaste of pain.

The brief joy a short meeting like this brings
is like seeing a roe deer in a field
as you pass it by quickly in the train.

Mirroring

Does she copy my quirks, my outstretched arm,
my verbal gambits and my turns of phrase?
I think she does; this joyful thought can raise
my sinking spirit in my inner storm.

Since her body language seems to conform
to mine, I take it as a sign of praise,
a flattery to set my heart ablaze
and change my lonely world from cold to warm.

Why copy the way I gesticulate
unless she has some feelings for me too?
This is surely proof that she could be mine.

Are they not sincere, those who imitate
and encode their affidavits to you?
In her gestures, am I thrown a lifeline?

15

The Ideal

If she has any flaws, I don't see them.
I find in her looks no imperfection,
in her manner no cause for objection,
nothing in her character to condemn.

My soul knows she is the crème de la crème,
with nothing that does not pass inspection,
from the peachiness of her complexion
to each strut of her well-proportioned frame.

The hemispheres of my brain have conspired
to idealise her and not to brook
any challenge to her supremacy.

I'm not in two minds about what's desired.
Even other beautiful girls who look
a bit like her appear ugly to me.

The A3 Lecture Theatre

Outside the A3 Lecture Theatre,
with my fellow first years I was waiting.
And my excitement was escalating
watching the second years come out of there.

One face was sure to be the face of her
and on each face I was concentrating.
My anticipation was translating
the hubbub into a fruit machine's whirr.

I saw her and her two friends spinning past,
three winning symbols. Could I catch her eye?
A nod from her would complete my rapture.

The reeling crowd of students moved too fast
and, without spotting me, she passed me by.
I was glum going into that lecture.

Inadequate Poet

Has there ever been a face in times past
as lovely as the face now loved by me?
Impossible to think that one could see
your graceful beauty topped, your looks surpassed.

It is clear to me that you've joined the cast
of history's beauties. I guarantee
your eminence. You cannot help but be
the star and all the others are outclassed.

Laura, Beatrice or Helen of Troy,
like them you have the power to inspire.
My mind's alight with hot, glittering rhymes.

Though just a glimpse of you is purest joy,
I'm not quite capturing what I desire.
I do you scant justice for future times.

Pot Noodle Man

I was a student of the things she did.
I'd watch her, discreetly, at a distance,
and as I monitored her existence,
I saw a disciplined, hard-working kid.

On the library's plush first floor I hid
as I placed the girl under surveillance.
I learned no secrets – but got some guidance.
One thing I noticed I thought was splendid:

She would eat an apple at eleven.
Was this why she looked healthier than me?
Pot Noodle Man was in poor condition.

Bad breath, plooks, acne pits, pale, unshaven,
how could I be a worthy devotee?
My teeth as well required much attention.

The Christmas Card

I decided to send a Christmas card.
I had to connect with her in some way.
I felt it was getting late in the day,
and months since we did the play by Stoppard.

She should know I hold her in high regard.
That was the thing I continued to say.
Be bold. Show her you have some vertebrae.
Send her a card. That wouldn't be too hard.

My head told me I was being a fool.
I didn't know her well enough for this.
My heart overruled my better judgement.

A poor token from one who wasn't cool –
an inarticulate *de profundis* –
to one to whom such things are doubtless sent.

20

Spring Semester

Back on campus after the winter break,
as I was walking back to AKD,
the cold making the loch a frozen sea
and vapours out of my sighs of heartache,

my numb self did a sudden double take.
In the distance and walking towards me,
a blonde-haired figure none other than she.
My feet through the footbridge sensed an earthquake.

I felt autistic, awkward, red-faced, green.
I said hello but had no more to say.
I didn't stop. She didn't seem to care.

I felt exposed, not wanting to be seen.
I wished right then that I was far away
and hadn't sent that Christmas card to her.

The All-Nighter

Drunk. Tired. It's four o' clock. That's 4 a.m.
I am watching that great film *The Third Man*.
I thought my friends would last but no-one can.
I'm all alone. There is no sign of them.

Nor of her. No sign of my precious gem.
Not at any point has her biggest fan
seen his love since this whole damn thing began.
Does she have the stamina for this game?

Going hither and zither from event
to event, it was so hard to endure
not spotting her. Did we pass in the dark?

But her absence at this screening has meant
I judge her taste in movies to be poor.
Against her name I place my one black mark.

22

Stirling University Campus

Strolling around the loch, seeing the tinge
of pink on the bark of a sycamore,
I think of her cheeks. My brain conjures more:
Her golden blonde hair, the Lady Di fringe,

slightly bulbous nose – which I wouldn't change –
hooded eyelids I can't help but adore,
her upper lip less full than her lower.
I, in my mind's eye, on her face impinge.

Grey squirrels are darting across the lawns,
emergency stops, quick changes of gear,
their undulating runs delighting me.

From the black of coots to the white of swans,
Love hones my vision as I now revere
the campus of this university.

Faintheart

I think to myself I should ask her out.
Time is passing and irons aren't so hot.
Do I think she fancies me? Maybe not.
I pray that she does but I'm filled with doubt.

Procrastination is what I'm about.
And I relish being tied in this knot,
an *i* who worships from afar a dot
and, strangely, feels both grubby and devout.

What happens if she turns down my invite?
Goodnight Vienna and Bonjour Tristesse.
I am very afraid of rejection.

I will put it off till the time is right,
until I feel the answer might be yes.
Right now I'm not sure of her affection.

Wheelchair Guy

I see her talking with the wheelchair guy,
a guy whose face is usually glum,
whose deep resentments you can never plumb,
who often scares me with his distant eye.

But he's smiling, he looks gentle and shy.
Today, I see that a new mood has come.
His eyes sparkle, his heart must be a drum.
I know what he's feeling and I know why.

I wonder if she knows what she provokes,
how her mere presence can give rise to joy?
It is a power that I've never had.

I don't have charm, I just have rubbish jokes,
the overuse of which tends to annoy.
I'm no joybringer, I make no-one glad.

The Doppelgänger

I never saw anyone harangue her.
She was treated with the utmost respect.
When guys spoke to her they were circumspect.
God forbid that they might drop a clanger!

I was jealous, not of the headbanger
who once talked to her trying to connect,
but of a bloke that I did not expect -
a lookalike, nay, my doppelgänger.

It was frightening how he looked like me.
A clone whose style was to communicate
with glib patter and jokes – at which she laughed.

What was in him but not in me to see?
Nothing, it transpired. They weren't intimate.
But while I thought they were, it drove me daft.

26

Terrible News

It was near to the end of semester.
I saw her, called out and she spoke to me.
She was more than usually happy.
Had she liked the way I had addressed her?

Could it be true that I now impressed her?
That she loved me, at least to some degree?
No. No. Her news, though it filled *her* with glee,
left *me* wondering what had possessed her.

She had a place on the student exchange
and was going to California,
to Santa Barbara to be exact.

I knew then next year would be sad and strange.
I'd be living in a dystopia.
I tried to look pleased. It was all an act.

27

Peasant Slave

So. That was it. I failed to ask her out
and now she'd be away for a whole year.
Perfect conditions for a sonneteer.
But for me right then it was a washout.

A bit like Hamlet, I'd been full of doubt
and dithered when my mission became clear.
Yet my peasant's knees shook when she was near
in silent hope I was in with a shout.

Did I take a chance and give it a go?
Did I dare to say what was in my heart,
that I wished that I could know her better?

The answer to all these questions is *No*.
But in an absent muse there's grist for art
and unborn sonnets find their begetter.

28

Flightpath

In September, on all the likely dates,
I gaze up into the infinite blue.
Am I watching the plane that carries you
across the North Atlantic to the States?

In these reveries that the mind creates,
I find myself up there where I pursue
the cruising jumbos and then try to view
the portholed face on which my heart fixates.

Although her flightpath is above my head
and she's in one of those jets in the sky,
my vision dissolves like a vapour trail.

I picture not her but nothing instead.
My fancy has nosedived; it won't comply.
In both real and imagined worlds I fail.

29

Santa Barbara

Of that far-off campus I cannot write.
I fancy the birds wake at dawn in bliss
and for a whole *annus mirabilis*
rejoice that there is where she spends the night.

Her inspiring looks must surely unite
ten thousand flautists in morning practice.
Oh, I'm a scorpion on a cactus
imagining scenes that are mighty trite.

If only I could see her, watch or spy
through the eyes of the tutors who teach her
or through the eyes of the man in the moon.

To glimpse her briefly as she passes by,
I'd take the form of the vilest creature –
a serpent surfacing in the lagoon.

30

Distance

You are out there in North America
and each day I'm compelled to think of you.
Love's soft centre rules, its colonels subdue
my sovereign state in a coup d'état.

Though I know that a great distance can mar
the strongest love, weakening it as do
wolves wearing down the weary caribou
running for its life in the cold tundra,

there's no chance the power of mere terrain
will wear out my love, kill it, or inter
my adoration of that absentee.

I would still fervently jump on a plane,
fly over the Rockies and surprise her
if I believed she ever thought of me.

31

The Weird Coincidence

A letter has come for my flatmate Pete.
He lays it on his dresser with a sigh.
He seems to dismiss it. I don't know why.
I look at it. My heart misses a beat.

This is so odd. Has there been some deceit?
The date, time and place has transfixed my eye.
Who knew that a postmark could terrify?
Santa Barbara stamped in letters neat.

The letter's from some girl he used to date
who loves him still; he claims he doesn't care.
I get the story from him later on.

I'm struck by Love's ironic duplicate.
Two students only got to go out there;
his girl and mine – but I keep mine unknown.

32

Tranquillity

Wisp of dense and lingering morning mist,
beautiful serenity's hieroglyph.
As it's fading away I wonder if
tranquillity and I can coexist.

Above the loch, the vapour flees our tryst,
unwilling to stay and hear my mischief,
the case against Love brought by a plaintiff
who can't find peace, a waspish pessimist.

I'm tired of dazzling Love's enduring hell
and long to return to a life that's dull
and set myself a realistic goal.

That I might though be worthy of my belle
is a notion I wish I could annul.
I'm in no-man's-land. I'm in a foxhole.

33

Sixteen Long Months

Sixteen long months have passed and she is back
at Stirling now. How long I've been waiting
for the moment that ends this frustrating
period in my private almanac!

Those months dragged. All I did was find the knack
of marking time, moping and stagnating,
dreaming about her and cultivating
the habits of a monomaniac.

I feared my love for her might fade away
when the time came for us again to meet.
Perhaps she'd changed and I would feel no thrill.

But outside the Cottrell Building today,
I spotted her. This fear is obsolete.
She's back, she's stunning and I love her still.

Roy Hattersley

I went along to hear Roy Hattersley
speak in the Logie Lecture Theatre.
A large crowd of students had turned up there.
I looked around to see what I could see.

My heart soared with joy unexpectedly
when my beady eyes came to rest on her.
And I thought I wasn't wrong to infer
some pleasure in her face when she saw me.

She raised her eyebrows and nodded her head
and flashed a genuinely sunny smile.
She mouthed a *hi* that I was pleased to get.

I can't remember what Hattersley said.
My attention was fixed across the aisle
and a few rows down – and would still be yet.

Extension

Far to the west, the pointed Ben Lomond
is the most glorious of all the hills.
Even its distance is something that thrills.
I feel this as well when I spot my blonde.

A feeling of which I am much too fond,
drowning in which is the source of my ills.
I need to act, learn some assertive skills,
not just behold but possess the beyond.

I need an extension on my essay
but how can I explain to my tutor
that I just can't focus on David Hume,

that thoughts of love are leading me astray?
Have pity on this dreamy-eyed suitor
and move the deadline to the crack of doom!

36

Grand Canyon

One night in the crowded Grange Disco Bar,
she came over to say hello to me.
On hearing the voice of this returnee,
I suddenly felt healed and up to par.

Warm and strong like a cup of café noir,
her voice reclaimed its place in my psyche.
I'd forgotten how gorgeous it could be,
more beautiful than the Spanish guitar.

She talked of her year in the USA.
How she would play volleyball on the beach.
I blushed as I pictured this in my mind.

The highlight for her was far and away
the Grand Canyon; beyond descriptive speech.
I promptly asked her to dance. She declined.

Continuous Assessment

I doubt if I have enough class for her.
My manners are rough, my vowels are flat.
I am too much this and not enough that.
I'm not quite what I think she's looking for.

I'm strangely neutral, neither happy nor
sad with this judgement. With one caveat.
The unlikelihood of a concordat
doesn't slam shut my wishful thinking door.

My rational mind does not have my ear.
The fantasist is immune to logic.
There are plain facts that he will just deny.

Suddenly a vision grips me with fear.
I foresee a fate that could be tragic.
This useless love for her may never die.

I Got You

Of all the songs that I loved dancing to
up at the Grange on a Saturday night,
one in particular was pure delight.
It was that Split Enz single – *I Got You*.

It was great – except I hadn't got you.
But the song had a power to excite,
the bass hitting that G would underwrite
my sense there was nothing I couldn't do.

It felt in that moment of potency
that I could connect, that I did belong
inside your blue-eyed world of golden hair,

and that if you were right now to join me
on the dancefloor with this ear-splitting song,
you'd find me attractive and debonair.

Paris, Texas

I am watching *Paris, Texas* tonight
and seated further down are her two friends.
And what the appearance of them portends
is my comet girl, that heavenly sight.

But even in the cinema's dimmed light,
it is clear the presence of her pals sends
a false message of lovely dividends.
She isn't here. She's somewhere else tonight.

A girl who doesn't seem to be a fan
of arthouse films and doesn't seem to drink.
Lacunae in my desideratum.

Is she my woman? Can I be her man?
If I ever ask her out then I think
it should be a meal, not to see a film.

The Library

In the distance, with the right apparel –
the scarlet polo neck and tight blue jeans –
a tiny figure amongst figurines
seeking the privacy of a carrel.

Outside, the sound of a Christmas carol
from singers with guitars and tambourines
with a fitting hallowedness supervenes.
Now the library is a cathedral.

She finds a free carrel, a monkish cell,
and studies for an hour and a half.
When she comes out I glimpse her from afar.

And then she's gone. A glimpse is magical
but how can such a brief thing be enough?
It's an appetiser. It's caviare.

Dissertation

I'm still in love, my heart is undeterred.
But my dream of love twists my scholar's fate.
I neglect my studies and at this rate
I am going to end up with a third.

Looking honestly at what has occurred,
the grades I've been getting have not been great.
Very few A's and none of them were straight.
I've been distracted. That can be inferred.

I'm majoring in her conversation.
Her scraps of news form scriptures in my head.
They comfort and support me like a crutch.

She's working hard on her dissertation.
Its subject is Virginia Woolf, she said.
Her adviser's not helping her that much.

42

The Friend

I had hitherto uttered not a word
about my secret love to anyone.
I tried to appear to be having fun,
to feign attraction to some other bird.

I was false with friends, shifty and absurd.
My truth was dumb once my lies had begun.
But with one good friend in a one-to-one,
my unredacted story became heard.

To this fine friend with the skill to demand
that I unburden myself of the load
that she saw was clearly weighing me down,

I confessed. I knew she would understand
the centripetal pull of the sad road
of love and not regard me as a clown.

43

Aborted Mission

Encouraged by the one friend I had told,
I decided I had to ask her out.
Excuses that I to myself would spout
no longer washed; I resolved to be bold.

Two and a half years. The iron was cold.
There had been no indication throughout
all that time that she could not live without
my love. Still, I would be going for gold.

I spied her in the library one night.
I was a lion eyeing a gazelle.
She sat at a bank of desks by herself.

But I couldn't advance. I froze in fright.
Her blonde mane was like an exploding shell.
Nerve-shot, I cowered behind a bookshelf.

Windsurfer on Airthrey Loch

Thinking of her, I stroll round Airthrey Loch,
past tall trees in my unassertive way.
The air is biting and the sky is grey.
It's hard to unwind. I regret this walk.

My psyche and the weather interlock.
Then a flapping noise, not too far away,
is heard. Rat-tat-tat. Drone of swishing spray.
A windsurfer's improvising pibroch.

With a beautiful triangular sail,
a bright red, white and royal blue design,
the board shoots through gunmetal waves with speed.

This windsurf rig is an assertive male,
mentored by a wetsuited Wittgenstein.
Whereof you catch the breeze, thereof proceed.

45

I Finally Ask Her Out

I asked her out. Finally. What a move!
In her usual seat, writing away,
she sat. But, unlike the previous day,
I didn't freeze. I had something to prove.

I marched towards her, slipped into a groove.
She tried to speak but I did not delay
in saying the line that I had to say
in a way no stage actor could improve.

She was, I could see from reading her face,
intent on ending this interaction.
She deftly gave a pro forma reply.

Clearly she had a procedure in place
when needing to take evasive action.
I loved her way of turning down a guy.

Unrequited Love

Unrequited love is the supreme gaffe.
It is to commit the most acutely
toe-curling, existential gaucherie
to mistake zero for your other half.

A zig zag printout from a seismograph
could not register the anomaly,
the magnitude of this catastrophe
of malfunctioning love, the shame, the faff.

I've had an abrupt reality check.
How could I have ever contemplated
that she could be mine, the mate of my soul,

kissing her pale, unattainable neck
and red, remote lips, or postulated
my square peg fitting into her round hole?

Aftermath of Dreams

I've experienced bliss and gone through hell
and some desolate stations in between.
Why did my heart choose her? What did it mean?
I didn't even know her very well.

I am no good at love, I don't excel.
I am always left with what might have been.
How could I have thought she could be my queen?
Why did it happen? It's so hard to tell.

Looking back on that last night of the play,
I maybe saw things that weren't in her eyes,
fooled myself and thought a romance was on.

How did I fail to see there was no way
that a guy like me could win such a prize?
Once that mistake was made, good sense was gone.

48

The ASH Party

At some function in Andrew Stewart Hall,
she turned up in a lovely turquoise dress.
I saw elegance and poise coalesce
in only one girl there, as I recall.

I felt I needed some more alcohol,
her presence putting me under some stress.
On her face there formed, well, a scowl, I guess.
She didn't want to see me there at all.

The sunny smile I'd loved could not be seen.
When our eyes chanced to meet, her glance was grim.
There was no misreading the signs this time,

no mistaking now what a look might mean.
I'd become literate, I wasn't dim.
I knew to talk would be a sort of crime.

Wallace Monument

I wish she wasn't still hanging around.
I wish Education students like her
did not do that extra ninth semester.
I feel like I want to live underground.

With her, I am toast and well overbrowned
and I do not want new ways to suffer.
I fear meeting her each time I venture
out for a walk or when I'm lecture-bound.

She's like that Wallace Monument that looks
down on you no matter where on campus
you are. All around I sense her presence.

In tutorials or reading my books,
I cannot escape her beauty's compass,
can never forget its opalescence.

50

Paradise

From this paradise I will be expelled
when my studies shortly come to an end.
I imagine this campus as my friend
and through my travails our friendship has held.

But, still, I'm no mystic. I have not quelled
my inner turmoil, nor managed to mend
my lovelorn heart, though on these paths I tend
to walk hoping to have these woes dispelled.

Would it not be better being a pine?
A serene tree that lives for centuries?
The pines don't pine nor passions misconceive.

They stand unmoved for years, they're always fine.
And I know as I'm hugging all those trees,
they'll feel no sadness when I have to leave.